365 Powerful Positive Affirmations for Black Women

Reprogram Your Mind to Boost Confidence,
Self-Esteem, Attract Success, Make Money,
Health, and Love

Layla Moon

Table of Contents

4 FREE Gifts

To help you along your spiritual journey, I've created 4 FREE bonus eBooks.

You can get instant access by signing up to my email newsletter below.

On top of the 4 free books, you will also receive weekly tips along with free book giveaways, discounts, and so much more.

All of these bonuses are 100% free with no strings attached. You don't need to provide any personal information except your email address.

To get your bonus, go to:

https://dreamlifepress.com/four-free-gifts

Or scan the QR code below

Spirit Guides for Beginners: How to Hear the Universe's Call and Communicate with Your Spirit Guide and Guardian Angels

Guided by Moon herself, inspired by her own experiences and knowledge that has been passed down by hundreds of generations for thousands of years, you'll discover everything you need to know to;

- Understanding what the call of the universe is
- How to hear and comprehend it
- Knowing who and what your spirit guides and guardian angels are
- Learning how to connect, start a conversation, and listen to your guides
- How to manifest your dreams with the help of the cosmic source
- Learning how to start living the life you want to live
- And so much more...

Law of Attraction: Manifest Your Desire

Learn how to tap into the infinite power of the universe and manifest everything you want in life.

Includes:

- Law of Attraction: Manifest Your Desire ebook
- Law of Attraction Workbook
- Cheat sheets and checklists so make sure you're on the right path

Hoodoo Book of Spells for Beginners: Easy and effective Rootwork, Conjuring, and Protection Spells for Healing and Prosperity

Harness the power of one of the greatest magics. Hoodoo is a powerful force ideal for holding negativity at bay, promoting positivity in all areas in your life, offering protection to the things you love, and ultimately taking control of your destiny.

Inside, you will discover:
- How to get started with Hoodoo in your day-to-day life
- How to use conjuration spells to manifest the life you want to live
- How casting protection spells can help you withstand the toughest of times
- Break cycles of bad luck and promote good fortune throughout your life
- Hoodoo to encourage prosperity and financial stability
- How to heal using Hoodoo magic, both short-term and long-term traumas and troubles
- Remove curses and banish pain, suffering, and negativity from your life
- And so much more…

Book of Shadows

A printable PDF to support you in your spiritual transformation.

Within the pages, you will find:

- Potion and tinctures tracking sheet
- Essential oils log pages
- Herbs log pages
- Magical rituals and spiritual body goals checklist
- Tarot reading spread sheets
- Weekly moon and planetary cycle tracker
- And so much more

Get all the resources for FREE by visiting the link below

https://dreamlifepress.com/four-free-gifts

Introduction

When was the last time you woke up and felt truly excited about the life you live? Are you living and thriving or just living and surviving? Would you like to change the narrative that has defined your life? Are you ready to become the best version of yourself and live your life to the fullest? If this is you, the key to unlocking that future is now in your hands... or mouth, so to speak. Change the words you speak and the life you seek will fall into place.

"Life is hard." "I can't do it." "I am no good." "I don't deserve this" ... These are just simple phrases that many of us use in our day-to-day life. What we don't know is the powerful impact these words have on our experiences. We need to undo the harm caused by those words through positive affirmations. This book, *365 **Powerful Affirmations for Black Women;*** *Reprogram Your Mind to Boost Confidence, Self-Esteem, Attract Success, Make Money, Health, and Love,* is everything you need to get started.

In this book, you will get:

- Fundamental teachings on how words shape your mindset and create the life you want

- Effective tips for activating the power of your affirmations

- Practical information for reprogramming your mind

- Words to affirm your expectations in the areas of love, health, wealth, and many more

- Powerful affirmations you can use for every single day of the year

This is not a one-and-done type of book. This is the book for every black woman looking to make her way in the world that we live in today. As a woman of color living in a society that sees people through lenses steeped in prejudice and biases, it can feel as though the scales are tipped against you from the start. I know how disheartening it feels when you are faced with disappointment again and again. But let me tell you something I wished someone told me when I was in your shoes.

You are not as powerless or as helpless as you think. You are capable of greatness far beyond what you've ever dreamed or imagined. You have the tools you need to shape your life. You can wake up to the life you have dreamed of. The first step on that journey is speaking the right words. This book, ***365 Powerful Affirmations for Black Women;*** *Reprogram Your Mind to Boost Confidence, Self-Esteem, Attract Success, Make Money, Health, and Love,* is the key to unlocking the power within.

So, take a deep breath. Exhale. Relax. You've got this. All you need to do is flip over to the next page and let your journey begin.

CHAPTER ONE

Preparing Your Mind

By now, you must have heard from several sources about how powerful the mind is. So, I am not going to go into details on that. My focus instead is to help you understand how you can utilize the power of your mind to your advantage through your words of affirmation. Before we get into that let me put out a disclaimer. Speaking the right words into your life is not going to create an overnight type of transformation. It took years of negative programming for you to get to your present experience and situation. To counteract that effect, you would need to give your words time to take root in your life.

Thankfully, you don't need an extended period to manifest your dreams through affirmations. The fact that you are being very conscious and deliberate about the words you speak to yourself and into your environment makes a world of difference in the outcome and how long it takes for that outcome to manifest. That being said, while transformation doesn't happen overnight, there are changes that take place every time you speak the right words. The end result is usually a culmination of all the changes. To prepare your mind to accept the words of affirmation that you speak, there are three things you must pay attention to. These three things are conviction, consistency, and commitment.

Conviction

According to the dictionary, conviction is a firm belief or opinion. Without conviction, when you speak those words of affirmation, they are as powerful as a feather drifting in the wind. They have no direction or purpose. Your conviction is what binds the words that you speak to the dreams that you have, making it an anchor that forces it to manifest in your life. When you have a strong belief in what you are saying, you become an unshakable force so that even when you are going through the darkest times, you will have the power to maintain your affirmations. Conviction is what gives you the courage to dream big dreams even though your circumstances may want to place limits on what you can achieve. The first step in preparing your mind for your affirmation journey is convincing yourself that the words you speak are your new reality. The moment you successfully achieve this, you become unstoppable.

Consistency

One mistake you cannot afford to make on your journey to manifesting the life you want is linking your affirmations to your mood. The words you speak to yourself must be constant and independent of how you feel. You cannot say I am amazing in one breath and then in the next call yourself a failure. You must be consistent in the words that you speak regarding your situation and how frequently you say it. Consciously or unconsciously, your mind has absorbed a lot of information through experiences, the people around you, and the words that they spoke to you. Some of that information may be hindering you from making advancements in specific areas of your life and so to unlearn those things, you need to consistently speak the right words. As I mentioned earlier, speaking words of affirmations is not something you do once and then forget about it. It must be done consistently over a long period. As you grow and evolve in life, the words may be tweaked and adjusted, but you should never stop speaking those things you want to manifest.

Commitment

It is imperative to ensure that the words you speak are backed up by actions. Let us say, for example, you are trying to manifest a specific type of house. Speaking that house into existence is only one-half of the equation. You need to take the necessary steps to back up your words. Taking the necessary steps doesn't mean you have to pay for the house right away. It could be something as simple as doing an internet search to find out how much a house like the one you are trying to manifest would cost. What you are doing when you take these little steps is physically aligning your actions with your affirmations. You can't be manifesting a house and yet take actions that make it look like you are passing up opportunities to make your dreams come true. Your actions show the level of commitment you have to the words that you have spoken. It doesn't matter if you're looking for a new job, a partner, or trying to get into the best shape of your life. The words that you speak to affirm the life you want to manifest must correspond with the actions that you take to make that affirmation your reality.

Tips on How to Use These Affirmations

A quick Google search will give you tons of tips on how to use affirmations and make them work for you faster. The tips I am going to share with you here are the ones that have worked for me. But before we get into that, I want you to understand that the timeline for manifesting your affirmations varies for different reasons. I have things that I manifested within days. I have those that took me over a year to come to light and then there are things that I am still affirming to this day. Does it mean that my affirmations are not working? No. There is a process to everything. Your affirmations create an alignment. Think of it as the individual stitches that come together to make up a fabric. The number of stitches you need depend on the length of fabric required for what you are trying to make. With this in mind, let us look at some of the things we can do to make those affirmations work faster.

1. A Positive Mindset

When I say a positive mindset, I am not referring to being upbeat and full of sunshine and rainbows. What I mean is that you need to be optimistic about the outcome. Whatever you are trying to affirm, you have to believe in its outcome and reality. No matter how big your dream or vision is, you must believe in the possibility of its manifestation. There is no compromising this. If for example you believe that you are going to triple your income in the coming months or years, you must see yourself achieving this; and this brings us to the next point.

2. Visualization

If you cannot see the words you are speaking in action, those words are empty. As humans, we tend to connect with things we can relate to our senses. When you can find a connection through your senses, you find conviction. Remember what I said about conviction and how it affects your affirmation? When you say, "I am beautiful," you need to see the beauty in yourself. The struggle we have with this part of our affirmation process is seeing ourselves through the eyes of other people. You need to stop building the image of yourself based on what other people think.

3. Be vocal

One critical mistake I made during my earlier affirmation years was reading my affirmations the same way I read a book. I read it to myself in silence. The very definition of an affirmation is speaking your expectations into existence. Without speaking out loud, you can't fulfill the terms of affirmation. The truth is this; the potency of the words you affirm takes its full form when you vocalize your intentions. This happens in two ways; one, it increases your ability to internalize the message which in turn affects your convictions positively. And two, you infuse energy into your atmosphere that communicates with the environment around you, and this helps to speed up the alignment of things to bring about the manifestation you seek.

These are simple but effective tools and tips to help you make the most of your affirmations. Your next step is to put them into practice and over the next 6 chapters, you will be getting 365 days' worth of affirmations covering key areas of your life. Remember, have Conviction. Be consistent. Be committed.

CHAPTER TWO

60 Affirmations for Confidence

Confidence is the backbone of everything that you do. To live the life you have only dreamed of, you must find the courage and confidence to do so.

1. In the face of everything that this day presents to me, I am bold and full of courage.

2. I stand firmly by what I hold true with utmost confidence and grace.

3. My voice cannot be muted by societal expectations. I speak up for myself.

4. I am confident in my skills, abilities, and potential.

5. I am made of greatness and strength, and I have the courage to back up my words with actions.

6. I can, and I will successfully complete every task I set out to achieve today.

7. I command the attention of everyone in any room I step into today because of my confidence.

8. In my speech, mannerisms, and deeds, I radiate positive confidence.

9. I tackle every project with the grace and efficiency that have become the markers of my confidence.

10. I am not afraid to embrace every facet of myself no matter how flawed I perceive them to be.

11. Today, I am better than I was yesterday, and tomorrow, I will be better than I am today.

12. I am breaking limits and surpassing every expectation in all my endeavors.

13. I choose to be excellent in everything that I set out to do.

14. I am not the mistakes I have made. I learn my lessons and grow.

15. I am the best version of myself regardless of what people say.

16. I am taking steps to conquer my fears and achieve my dreams.

17. I am not going to stand in the way of my success. I believe in the power of me.

18. I am the leading lady in my own life. No one is going to upstage me.

19. My confidence is made of more than the clothes I wear or the things I own.

20. The opinions of other people can never diminish my confidence and faith in myself.

21. I trust my instincts and therefore every emotion I experience is valid.

22. I am a queen, a boss and a divine being in every way that defines those words.

23. I am confident in the person I am today and in the person I will become tomorrow.

24. I am confident enough to cast aside my insecurities to give room for other queens to shine.

25. I am uniquely built to handle whatever challenges or obstacles stand in my way today.

26. I am proud of every single thing I have achieved, whether big or small.

27. I deserve every bit of happiness and positivity that comes my way today.

28. I accept myself for who I am, and this does not make me any less or better than anyone else.

29. I am authentic and uniquely myself wherever I am and this makes me feel powerful.

30. I am not afraid to take the necessary steps to become a better version of myself.

31. I relentlessly pursue my goals with fierce determination and absolute conviction.

32. I am a woman of substance and character. I don't need to seek validation from anyone except me.

33. Life does not happen to me. I am happening to life because I am in charge of my life.

34. I am taking charge of my life today and I won't be needing anyone's permission to be amazing.

35. I am making good and morally sound decisions that prioritize my physical and mental wellbeing.

36. I am smart enough to know what is right for me and I am confident enough to pick myself first.

37. I am not afraid to prioritize my wants, needs, and expectations in whatever relationship I am in.

38. Neither my hair, my clothes, the color of my skin, nor my social status has the power to define or authenticate my person.

39. I refuse to diminish my light or dumb down my potential just to make other people feel better about themselves.

40. I am attracting people who genuinely desire to see me succeed and are not threatened by the absolute confidence I have in myself.

41. I am surrounded by a positive force field that reinforces my confidence and protects my ability to be myself.

42. I am a light that burns brightly and I am capable of illuminating my world.

43. I am protected from the antagonism and bullying that is pervasive online and offline. It does not and cannot change me.

44. I work and function in the sound knowledge of who I am; nothing can distract me from my true identity.

45. I acknowledge the fears and concerns that I have, and I take the necessary precautions to avoid a negative outcome. I refuse to let those fears control me.

46. I am always in charge of my life, even when things appear out of control.

47. There is no limit on my ability to go out into the world, conquer my fears, and live out my dreams.

48. The world is my runway and I am confidently strutting in with grace, charm, and charisma.

49. I have the power to create my dreams and deliver on them.

50. I am not going to second guess or put myself down just because I am trying to fit into the image of what other people expect me to be.

51. I am communicating my feelings and thoughts in a way that sincerely conveys the message I want to pass across to whoever is listening.

52. I deserve every accolade, compliment, or award that comes my way today because I have earned it.

53. I am done with underestimating my potential and skills. I am constantly speaking to my strengths.

54. I am stepping into my best life and I am not going to question any of the good or positive experiences I have today.

56. I am ready and qualified for the next level of greatness in my life. I close the door to mediocrity and redundancy.

57. I am rocking my role as a sister, daughter, wife, friend, business owner, worker, and as a woman generally. I am doing a great job.

58. I can make a difference in my world, and I am taking that first step today.

59. I am the woman I want to be; brave, bold, and different.

60. I believe in my dreams and in my ability to make them my reality.

61. I am delivering excellence in everything I do.

CHAPTER THREE

60 Affirmations for Self-Esteem

Your self-esteem is an echo of the perception you have about yourself. It fuels your confidence which in turn drives your confidence. A woman who knows who she is and what she is worth cannot be brought down easily. Give your self-esteem a boost and watch yourself rise/grow in every area of your life.

1. I am black. I am beautiful. I am brilliant. I am powerful. I am everything I need to thrive in this life.

2. I love the curves and lines of my body because they illuminate my womanhood and amplify my uniqueness.

3. I am me and that is enough. I don't need to be anyone else.

4. I listen to my positive inner voice. My views about myself are the only views that matter.

5. I am the new normal. I am breaking every cycle of abuse that has haunted the women in my family.

6. I am happy and I am actively focusing on my health and well-being to maintain my happiness today.

7. I am more than my circumstance or experience. I am made of more.

8. I am a victor. I am a survivor. I am a winner.

9. I am excited because I have so much to look forward to today.

10. I am free to be whoever I want and I am exercising this freedom.

11. I am proud of the woman I see in the mirror every day.

12. I believe in the work I am putting in to make myself better.

13. I am making progress in my efforts to be my best self.

14. I am attracting the kind of friendships and relationships that uplift me.

15. I am a beautiful black woman pursuing her dreams and I am well-equipped for this journey.

16. I am shutting out any voice that demeans my person and relevance.

17. I am important. I matter to the people in my world.

18. I am taking full ownership of my life. I am in the driver's seat now.

19. I am worthy of the love, respect, and affection I desire.

20. I am talented, resourceful, and emotionally capable of attaining all my goals.

21. I am my own standard of beauty. I embrace the features that differentiate me from every other woman.

22. My beauty is exquisite. My body is divine. My heart is a treasure trove of wonders.

23. I am in love with everything about me. My looks, my personality, my ambitions... they excite me.

24. I am done tolerating people who have no regard for my person or my values. I demand respect.

25. I am kind, sensitive, and vulnerable. I am willful, direct, and incredibly strong. All these different sides of myself make me powerful.

26. I am not a second option type of woman. I prioritize myself, so I expect to be prioritized.

27. I respect myself enough to avoid situations that negatively affect my mental health, physical health, or brand.

28. I am a sexual and sensual creature. I have no reason to be ashamed or embarrassed by this.

29. I am courageously walking out of any unhealthy alliances or relationships that threaten my peace and sanity.

30. I am stronger, wiser, and better than the person people have painted me out to be. I will not conform to their expectations.

31. I am the prize. I am the pot of gold at the end of the rainbow. Any person I date is lucky to be chosen.

32. I am beautiful inside and out.

33. I am perfectly okay with the fact that I am not meant for everyone.

34. I acknowledge the reality that people's perception of me is not my problem to solve.

35. My body, with its scars, changes, and stretch marks, is a magnificent piece of art. I appreciate its beauty and perseverance.

36. I am imperfectly perfect the way I am, and I love that about myself.

37. I am seen. I am heard. I am loved. I am accepted.

38. I honor my body by choosing to engage in healthy habits that promote my physical well-being.

39. My confidence in myself gets better every day. I am patient with the process.

40. I am my own special hype woman and cheerleader. I don't talk myself down.

41. I am kind and forgiving to myself, especially when it comes to the mistakes I make.

42. I am completely in love with my magnificent brown skin and how it always makes me feel beautiful.

43. I radiate light, and I refuse to add my voice to the crowd of negative voices around me.

44. I am a constant work in progress. My goal is not perfection. My goal is to be better than the person I was yesterday.

45. I am okay with being different. My identity as a woman is not based on other people's opinions of what I should look like.

46. I take full ownership of my happiness. I am done waiting on other people to make me happy.

47. I am a goddess in human form and I manifest divinity through my words, thoughts, and actions.

48. I am aware of the power behind my words and therefore, today, I am choosing to use words that build me up.

49. I am a brave queen. I can stand up to my challenges. I am not waiting for anyone to rescue me.

50. I deserve to be pampered, protected, and pleasured.

51. I am never going to quit on myself. I owe it to myself to see my goals to the finish line.

52. My failures, pain, and trauma are part of the bricks I will piece together to build my empire.

53. I am talented at what I do. I offer tremendous value to any organization I choose to work for.

54. I am uprooting every lie planted in my soul that undermines my worth. I am replacing those lies with the truth about myself.

55. I am opening up to access the power and strength I have within me.

56. I am built for this time and season. Nothing is too tough for me to handle.

57. I am not only going to survive this season, I will thrive in this season.

58. I am not going back to people or circumstances that held me back. I am moving onward and forward.

59. I am stepping up and showing up for myself today.

60. I enjoy the woman I am today.

61. I embrace uniqueness and power as a beautiful melanated black queen.

CHAPTER FOUR

60 Affirmations for Attracting Success

Success means different things to different people. Just remember, success does not mean total perfection or the absence of challenges. But at the end of the day, when you are in a space where you have mental balance, financial abundance, and strong alliances, it is safe to say that you are successful.

1. I am attracting wealth and abundance into my life.

2. I am experiencing tremendous growth in every area of my life.

3. I am forming alliances and building lasting relationships that provide me with safety and comfort.

4. I am engaging in new habits that adequately prepare me for a life of success.

5. I am moving out of my comfort zone and conquering new territories.

6. I embody success.

7. My actions, choices, and thoughts are aligned with the person I want to become.

8. I can get it all; the career I enjoy, the love that makes me glow, the family that supports me, and the abundance that brings me peace.

9. I am taking steps today to guarantee the future I desire.

10. I have the code to unlock my success story.

11. I have all the resources I need to make my dreams a

reality.

12. I am taking advantage of every opportunity that comes my way today.

13. I am meant for bigger things in life. I refuse to stay small.

14. I am done eating the scraps that fall off other people's table. I am building my own table.

15. I am sharing my energy with people who aspire for greater levels of success. I refuse to engage with mediocrity.

16. My morning rituals set me up perfectly for a successful day.

17. I am speaking words that activate the goal-getter in me.

18. I am reading books and listening to content that help me build a success mindset.

19. I am taking actions that lead me to success.

20. I am open to learning from my mistakes and

implementing strategies that turn those mistakes into stepping rungs on my success ladder.

21. I am deactivating those triggers that cause me to sabotage myself every time I get closer to my goals.

22. I am consistent and diligent in the habits that bring about success in my life.

23. I am upgrading my mindset to match the life I want to live.

24. I am unlearning negative patterns of behavior that have held me from reaching my full potential.

25. I am navigating life like a person who has purpose and direction. My days of stumbling around are over.

26. I am making a big investment in myself because I recognize the fact that I am my biggest asset.

27. I am readjusting my priorities and pushing strongly for my goals.

28. I am successful.

29. I am not giving up until I get the life I want.

30. I know what I am worth and what I bring to the table. I am not going to settle for less. I will get what I want.

31. I am working hard and making the necessary sacrifices for the life I want.

32. I am building a healthy space for me to thrive mentally, physically, and financially.

33. My success is positively impacting my world.

34. I am loving how positive and powerful I have become.

35. I am bigger than any anxiety, doubts, or negative opinions about my success.

36. I have the right attitude for success and I am choosing that today.

37. I am pouring my energy into building the future I desire.

38. I am selecting projects, people, and opportunities that are in alignment with my aspirations.

39. I am actively engaging in things that lead me to my success goals.

40. I deserve and have earned every success milestone I cross.

41. I am working with the knowledge that life is happening for me today.

42. I am a woman of action. I am executing my tasks more than I am making excuses.

43. I am balanced in my pursuit of success. I rest when I need to. I play when I need to, and I work when I need to.

44. I am taking responsibility for how my success story plays out. I am not giving that power to anyone.

45. I am crushing all my goals and bringing myself closer to my dreams.

46. I am attracting people who are genuinely interested in seeing me succeed.

47. I believe in myself and my ability to make my success aspirations a reality.

48. I am taking pleasure in the simple moments I find on my journey to the top.

49. I am refusing to let my emotions dictate how much work I put into my growth.

50. I am not competing with anyone when it comes to my success story. The position at the top is meant for me.

51. I am not threatened by the successes of other women. I celebrate their victories and allow them to inspire me.

52. I have the courage to outgrow my past and become the woman I want to be even if it might mean letting go of habits, people, or situations.

53. I have a plan for my future and I am going to make it happen no matter what.

54. I am walking into the most successful season of my life and I am ready for it.

55. I am ready to elevate myself and become better at what I do.

56. I open myself up to receive abundance. I accept love in abundance, wealth in abundance, and health in abundance.

57. I am in control of how much effort I put into achieving my goals. I work with this mindset every day.

58. I am not afraid, ashamed, or anxious about asking for more. I deserve it.

59. I am valuable enough to attract the level of success I want.

60. My dreams are a possible reality and I am attracting the right people, opportunities, and elements to make my dreams my reality.

61. I am wealthy in the things that matter to me.

CHAPTER FIVE

60 Affirmations for Making Money

Money is a form of wealth. The attitude we have towards money makes a world of difference in how we experience it. These affirmations can help you build a healthier and more productive relationship with money.

1. Money works for me and not the other way round.

2. I am attracting the kind of opportunities that allow me to double the returns on my investments.

3. I have a healthy attitude towards money and as a result, I use it wisely.

4. I am making the right financial choices. I am done with financial lack or absence.

5. I have created multiple streams of income for wealth to flow through. I can never be broke.

6. I am resourceful in how I create and distribute wealth.

7. I have a success mindset and this attracts wealth.

8. In all my business endeavors, I am a money magnet.

9. I am strategically positioned to create and accumulate wealth.

10. Abundance and wealth is a natural state for me.

11. I am reaping tremendous financial rewards for all the hard work I put in.

12. I am bold in my desire to be rich and I have set plans in motion to help me achieve this.

13. I am creating wealth opportunities for myself and the people around me.

14. I am breaking every financial limit in my family and exceeding our financial projections and expectations.

15. I am a wealth creator.

16. My habits have strong financial value. My daily actions have strong links to the amount of wealth I accrue.

17. I have unlocked the level of wealth that is capable of catering to all my needs.

18. The scales are tipped in my favor to ensure abundance and wealth in my life.

19. I am building the type of wealth that lasts for generations.

20. My wealth is positively impacting the people in my life, my community, and my world.

21. I am living in immense financial abundance every single day.

22. I have the financial capacity to buy whatever I want.

23. I am financially free. I have paid off all my debts.

24. I am open to receiving money from both expected and unexpected sources.

25. I am doing what I enjoy, living my best life, and creating wealth in the process.

26. I have an unending financial source that guarantees a secure income.

27. I am creating financially profitable business ventures.

28. I am rich in every resource required to help me build sustainable wealth.

29. I am building empires with high-income yields.

30. I am creating relationships that boost my network portfolio.

31. The people I have in my circle have a success mindset that inspires me to reach for my goals.

32. I am a successful wealth manager.

33. I am wise and I have the ability to convert the resources at my disposal into viable streams of income.

34. I am building the kind of financial profile that makes me an asset in any economy.

35. I am growing my wealth from a place of rest.

36. I am not chasing after money. Money is chasing after me.

37. I will enjoy the financial benefits of all my hard work.

38. My brain is wired to see the wealth creation opportunities in any situation.

39. I am making money moves today to build a stable financial future for myself.

40. I am bold in my decision to grow and acquire more wealth.

41. I am a living expression of the phrase, "smiling to the bank."

42. I am attracting the kind of jobs that give me financial freedom and job fulfillment.

43. I know how to enjoy the money that comes my way. I spend wisely.

44. Every form of promotion that comes my way today brings financial advancement as well.

45. I am not degrading or devaluing myself for financial opportunities.

46. I deserve every good thing that life has to offer, including financial abundance.

47. I am experiencing exponential financial growth today.

48. I have access to the right people who can positively impact my financial story.

49. I can afford the lifestyle that I desire with ease.

50. There is no limit to what I can achieve financially.

51. I am setting financial goals that are on the same frequency as my vision for the future.

52. I am creating a new chapter in my financial story today.

53. I am going to get the amount of money I need to live the life I desire.

54. I have the money touch. Every venture I put my hands on turns into a highly profitable business.

55. I have become the mistress of money. I have absolute control over my financial outcome.

56. My income can never be less than my expenses.

57. I am living the life I dreamed of every day because I am financially free.

58. I am making serious money off my skills, talents, and ideas.

59. I am a multi-millionaire in different currencies of the world.

60. I am intentional about how I make and spend my money.

61. I can find ways to create wealth even in unexpected places.

CHAPTER SIX

60 Affirmations for Health

Health, as they say, is wealth. Without good health, it is almost impossible to enjoy all the amazing gifts that life has to offer. Poor health puts a limit on the standard of a person's quality of life. Through these affirmations, you can manifest sound health.

1. I am healthy in body, mind, and spirit.

2. Every system, organ, and cell in my body is functioning at maximum capacity for the promotion of my well-being.

3. My body is in the best condition right now and I am appreciative of this.

4. Thanks to my sound mind and body, I am physically fit and strong.

5. I am in a harmonious place spiritually and this provides me with peace and clarity.

6. My mind is a vast fertile field beaming with positive energy and radiating positive thoughts.

7. The physical limitations placed on my body do not stop me from enjoying and living my life to the fullest.

8. My body and mind are at peak performance every single day.

9. I am experiencing spiritual enlightenment that elevates my mind and stabilizes my body.

10. I feel good about the body I am in because I am perfect by my standards.

11. I honor my body by engaging in practices that promote my physical and mental well-being.

12. I am creating the right atmosphere for me to live a healthy life.

13. I am paying serious care to my health by investing in the right things for my body.

14. I exercise right. I eat right. I also take the required amount of rest to keep myself in great shape.

15. I am partnering with the right people to help ensure that my health remains in prime condition.

16. The people in my circle are working together with me to protect my overall health.

17. My body is healing and recovering from any trauma it has suffered in the past.

18. I have a divine layer of protection that ensures my mind and body do not fall victim to any plague or disease.

19. My age, genetic makeup, gender, or social beauty standards do not define my health profile.

20. My mind and body connection is in sync and this puts me in excellent physical condition.

21. I am a medical marvel and the excellent state of my physical health as well as the high standard of my quality of life continues to baffle experts in the medical community.

22. My immune system is strong enough to fight off infections and keep diseases at bay.

23. The food I eat sustains me and provides sufficient nutrients for my body to stay healthy for longer.

24. I have a sound body and a clear mind.

25. My spiritual energy is in complete alignment with my health goals and strategies.

26. I intuitively know the right foods for my body and the right exercises to help me reach my health goals.

27. I take my health seriously. It is at the very top of my to-do list.

28. All my daily habits and activities support my mind and body goals.

29. I am consistent in the habits that are meant to keep me physically fit.

30. I love my body enough to make healthier choices every single time.

31. I am expecting an unending stream of health and vitality into my mind and body.

32. I am exercising the power I have to make good choices for my physical and mental wellbeing.

33. I am capable of managing emotions like anxiety, anger, and pain. They do not control me.

34. I am immersed in a sphere that keeps me in a safe environment for my mental health to thrive.

35. I am not subscribing to fashion fads and practices simply because they are trendy. I focus on things that actually help me.

36. I am willing and ready to put in the physical and mental work needed for me to stay in good shape.

37. The goals I create for my body are designed to appeal to me. I am not trying to please anyone.

38. My body and mind are mine to command. I do what I want and what I want is what is best for my body.

39. I am stepping up all efforts to be the best version of myself.

40. I enjoy the activities I engage in to promote my physical wellbeing.

41. I have the mental capacity to persevere through my physical routines and maintain a fit body.

42. I am a sexy black woman with a hot body and a sound mind.

43. Regardless of how I feel, I am getting out of bed and pushing myself to be physically fit.

44. I am finding the motivation within myself to be healthy in mind and body.

45. I wake up every morning with renewed strength and vigor.

46. I feel very good today. I am in the right body and mindset.

47. Today, I will choose myself. When I am presented with tempting offers that might derail me, I choose what is best for me.

48. I celebrate myself for surviving the bullets life has shot at me. I have become mentally strong because of it.

49. I am craving healthy foods and habits that improve me physically and mentally.

50. I am patient with the progress I am making on my fitness journey.

51. My body is designed to do amazing things like get me through the day, provide pleasure, birth life, and so on. I honor the work it does.

52. I am honoring the sacrifices my body makes by ensuring that I nourish it with a balanced diet, exercise routines, and content that helps me mentally and physically.

53. I have an excellent health care team that works together to guarantee that I am financially, mentally, and physically able to stay in good shape.

54. I attract like-minded people who share similar health goals and take actions that inspire/motivate me to keep chasing my goals.

55. I am transforming my body into a living, breathing version of my vision board.

56. From the clothes I wear to the food I eat, I am consciously choosing the things that make me look and feel good.

57. I am attracting the energy I need to complete my fitness routines today.

58. Putting myself first and prioritizing my health gets me very excited.

59. I am welcoming support, encouragement, and positivity into my wellbeing journey.

60. The different parts of my body that make me whole are imperfect pieces coming together to fit perfectly. I love my body.

61. My health is a part of my wealth and I have it in abundance.

CHAPTER SEVEN

60 Affirmations for Love

Everyone deserves love. Love is at the center of everything that we do. Love for people. Love for self. Passion for life. These are all different expressions of love and we all need it in our lives.

1. I welcome this day with love in my heart, warmth in my soul, and light in my eyes.

2. I am made for the safe, warm, and everlasting type of love that I crave.

3. I deserve to be loved and nurtured.

4. I have a lot of love to give and I am connecting with the kind of people who deserve my love.

5. My heart is open to giving and receiving healthy love.

6. I am attracting people who genuinely love and care for me.

7. I am healing from the pains from my past and opening up my heart to opportunities to find genuine love.

8. My love is authentic and powerful.

9. My love is pure and true.

10. I am a prime expression of love in human form.

11. I am involved in relationships that fuel my love tank.

12. I respect and respond to the dynamics of my relationship, as long as it is positive.

13. I am setting and enforcing healthy boundaries in my relationships.

14. I am experiencing the most amazing kind of love every day.

15. I love myself with fierce devotion and compassion.

16. The energy I give out today is attracting my soulmate to me.

17. I am in a season of abundant love, peace, and happiness.

18. I refuse to let the traumas of my past decide my next steps for the future.

19. I am not burdening my current relationships with the emotional baggage from my previous relationships.

20. I am establishing intimate connections that help me find love within and around me.

21. I recognize relationships that are healthy for me and I seek them out.

22. My love antenna is tuned in to a higher frequency to attract people operating at the same level.

23. I am letting go of my past emotional struggles and conquering my fears.

24. I forgive people who have hurt me deeply with their words and actions.

25. I release myself from the bondage of pain, anger, and fear that has held me back from knowing true love.

26. I am walking into the starting point of the best days of the rest of my life.

27. I am not spending my days waiting for love to find me.

28. I am giving myself the love, care, and attention that I need.

29. Today, I am falling deeply in love with myself all over again.

30. I am loving myself without conditions or expectations.

31. My love is wholesome, unconditional, and forgiving.

32. I naturally avoid people with a tendency to manipulate and take advantage of my love.

33. I am taking on projects that I love. This gives me an enjoyable work experience.

34. I am finding love in the simple things that I do every day.

35. I am exuding an aura that attracts love into my life.

36. I repel people who are negative, pessimistic, and have no good intentions towards me.

37. I am open about waiting for people to earn my love and trust before I make any commitment, especially in romantic partnerships.

38. I am not repeating the same mistakes from my past relationships.

39. I forgive myself and I choose to embrace my flaws and my strengths.

40. My life is characterized by love.

41. I am committed to living the life I love.

42. I am releasing love into the universe and the universe is giving it back to me in return.

43. I am powerful because I recognize the power of having strong self-love.

44. I know my worth and I am attracting the kind of people who know my worth too.

45. I am not settling for any relationship that offers less than what I deserve.

46. I can see the life that I want clearly, and I am actively in pursuit of it.

47. I am allowing myself to become a vessel through which love flows into the lives of the people around me today.

48. The love in my romantic life is rejuvenated and made brand new.

49. My romantic partner and I are in a stable and healthy love relationship with ourselves and each other.

50. I am experiencing renewed bonds of deep and genuine friendships.

51. I have outgrown habits that sabotage my love relationships.

52. My love grows and finds expression in different ways every day.

53. I am grateful for the kind, committed, and loving partner I have.

54. I am letting go of relationships that no longer serve me and opening myself to ones that do.

55. My love is life-giving, life-transforming, and entirely wholesome. It is a positive powerful force.

56. My journey to my happily ever after begins today, and I am completely ready for it.

57. I am the key to my happiness, and I am unlocking that door to usher in my season of abundant joy.

58. I am investing myself in the right relationships and giving my love to those who deserve it.

59. My love is changing me from the inside and transforming me into the woman I have dreamed of becoming.

60. I am done with stagnated relationships and I am choosing to seek out opportunities to grow in love.

61. Love is a constant presence in my heart, home, and life.

Conclusion

The book is almost at the end. However, you are just beginning your journey. I am honored to have started this process with you but don't let it end here. Speak your affirmations loudly and clearly until these words drown out those voices that belittle your potential and undermine the effort you have put into becoming the person that you are today. You know somewhere deep down inside that you were made for more than this. Now is the time to prove it.

Connect with your affirmations. Rewrite them to align with your expectations if you have to, but never stop speaking those affirmations. Regardless of your religious affiliation or cultural roots, the power behind the words you speak to yourself is real. Will it teleport you to your desired destination within seconds? Absolutely not. But will it get you there eventually? Absolutely yes. Become more conscious and deliberate about what you say and how you say it. The rest will fall into place.

Before I jump into the goodbyes, I want you to know that you have access to the keys that will bring you the life you deserve. All you have to do is commit to it, be consistent with it, and hold on to your convictions. Being a black woman in today's society can be a blessing or a curse. Thankfully, you get to decide on what spectrum you fall under. Pick a side, build your vision, and speak it into existence.

That said, my part here is done. I look forward to reading your success story. So don't forget to write and share the details of your journey. Until then, be deliberate about changing your life for the better.

Thank You

Before you go, I just wanted to say thank you for purchasing my book.

There are many books on the same topic, but you took a chance and chose this one.

So, thank you for choosing me and for reading this book all the way to the end.

Now, I wanted to ask you for a small favor. **Could you please consider posting a review for the book? Reviews are the easiest way to support an independent author like me.**

Your feedback will help me continue to create books that will help you achieve the results you want. So, if you enjoyed it, please let me know.

Image - vecteezy.com

www.ingramcontent.com/pod-product-compliance
Lightning Source LLC
Chambersburg PA
CBHW071217120626
46546CB00006B/2606